W9-DAF-114

I Built A Bridge & Other Poems

I Built A Bridge

And Other Poems

By David B. Steinman

The Davidson Press
* publishers *
New York 1955

Upsala College
Library
East Orange, N. J.

Copyright 1955 by The Davidson Press

FIRST EDITION

A number of the poems in this collection appeared originally
in the New York Times, American Engineer, The Bent,
Partners, The Manhattan Quarterly, Boston Post, American
City, Hartford Courant, Australasian Engineer, etc.

811.5
S823i

91821

Printed in the United States of America

FOR MY WIFE

Eternity is all too brief to prove
the wonder and the glory of your love

Introduction

THE AUTHOR of *I Built A Bridge & Other Poems* is one of the world's most famous bridge engineers and consultants. The mere listing of bridges of his design in both hemispheres requires more than a column in that space-chary publication *Who's Who in America*. Honorary degrees, citations, awards, too many to enumerate, have come to him from universities, societies and municipalities, here and abroad, in recognition of his outstanding achievements.

In this modest volume, however, David B. Steinman has sought another form of creative outlet. For him poetry has proved a delightful avocation, a rewarding pursuit. It has given him the opportunity to express his philosophy of life, to reveal his sentiments, to note his many impressions of man and nature. Whether he deals with bridges as spiritual and social symbols of a new and higher level of civilization, or with love and the bitter-sweet of its many manifestations, or with religion as a life force, or with nature and people, he does so with unquestioned sincerity. Through his verses the reader may recognize the man who wrought them, a great constructive genius who has not forgotten that he is primarily a human being, one who strives to live in accordance with the ideal set forth in Micah 6, 8: "What doth the Lord require of thee, but to do justly, and to love mercy, and to walk humbly with thy God?"

Poetry to Steinman is what the violin was to the late Albert Einstein, a reminder that the dreams, ideals and visions of man lie beyond the power of formula or blueprint to record.

Elias Lieberman

Contents

The Song Of The Bridge

With hammer-clang on steel and rock
    I sing the song of men who build.
With strength defying storm and shock
    I sing a hymn of dreams fulfilled.

I lift my span, I fling it wide,
    And stand where wind and wave contend.
I bear the load so men may ride
    Whither they will, and to what end.

The light gleams on my strands and bars
    In glory when the sun goes down.
I spread a net to hold the stars
    And wear the sunset as my crown.

I Built A Bridge

I built a bridge across the tide
   To gain the farther shore,
And there I came on fairer glens
   Than any glimpsed before.

I built a bridge across a vale
   To reach the upland slope;
With singing heart I built the span —
   A rainbow arch of hope.

I built a bridge across a gulf
   To hail my fellow man;
I found in him a kindred spark —
   He helped me build the span.

I built a bridge across the years
   To win tranquillity;
I did not know how beautiful
   The last of life could be.

I built a bridge across the dark
   To touch the shores of light,
And faith it was that sped me on,
   And love that gave me sight.

A Dream, A Song, A Prayer

A bridge of strength and grace in mystic blend
Embodies spirit treasures that transcend
The steel and stone; the builder's dream is there,
Each curve a song, each soaring line a prayer.
A dream, a song, a prayer — these three combine
To make the bridge a beacon and a shrine.

So with our lives, O Builder of our Span,
Help us to weave these strands into Thy plan
In trinity: a dream to point the goal;
A song to cheer; a prayer to lift the soul.
Grant us these gifts to cherish and to share;
Give us the living dream, the song, the prayer.

Ad Astra

When man first flung a log astride a stream,
He leapt millenniums beyond his birth;
Now strands of steel translate his lofty dream
To link the farthest corners of the earth;
He tames the sea, and ventures forth to sail
The very skies in globe-encircling flight;
His jets and rockets blaze a fiery trail
And ring the universe with lanes of light.

Unsated still, though master now of space,
Man strives (as strive he must) to conquer time;
Some inner force impels him on, to trace
Beyond the stars a destiny sublime.
    With light of faith to set his spirit free
    Man builds a bridge to span eternity.

Help Me, Lord,
To Build My Span

Anchored firm in solid rock,
  On Thy foundation let me build —
Strong to bear each strain and shock,
  An arch of dreams and faith fulfilled.

Help me, Lord, to build my span
  Across the chasm of the years;
Firm in purpose, true in plan,
  Above the drag of doubt and fears.

Help me to build on Thy high road
  A bridge to serve the common good;
To smooth the way and lift the load,
  A link of human brotherhood.

The Bridge

In days gone by, a valiant band
With consecrated heart and hand
Set out as pilgrims, seeking ways
To clear the wilderness of fear,
To bring the distant places near,
To build new roads to brighter days.

The pilgrims built a bridge of wood:
In massive strength the great span stood.
But ere the bridge with load was strained,
A flaming spark fell on the span,
A holocaust of dread began . . .
Then naught but glowing ash remained.

The pilgrims labored to atone:
This time they built a bridge of stone.
But ere the builders' thrill had waned,
An earthquake heaved and split the ground,
Felling the bridge with crashing sound . . .
Then naught but rubble heap remained.

Yet undiminished in their zeal
The pilgrims built a bridge of steel.
But as their eyes aloft were trained,
A thing of terror, hurtling past,
Dissolved the bridge in fission blast . . .
Then naught but vapor mist remained.

But in the pit of their despair
There came an answer to their prayer:
As clouds rolled back before their gaze,
A radiant vision met their eyes —
A prismed span across the skies,
Resplendent in its glowing rays.

And as they watched with wonder high,
They heard a Voice speak from the sky:
"To span the gap from man to man
Construct a bridge not made by hands,
Not wood or stone or iron bands —
Of Human Kindness build the span!"

Brooklyn Bridge: Nightfall

Against the city's gleaming spires,
  Above the ships that ply the stream,
A bridge of haunting beauty stands —
  Fulfillment of an artist's dream.

From deep beneath the tidal flow
  Two granite towers proudly rise
To hold the pendent strands aloft —
  A harp against the sunset skies.

Each pylon frames, between its shafts,
  Twin Gothic portals pierced with blue
And crowned with magic laced design
  Of lines and curves that Euclid knew.

The silver meshings of the net
  Are beaded with the stars of night
Like jeweled dewdrops that adorn
  A spiderweb in evening light.

Between the towers reaching high
  A cradle for the stars is swung;
And from this soaring cable curve
  A latticework of steel is hung.

Around the bridge in afterglow
  The city's lights like fireflies gleam,

And eyes look up to see the span —
A poem stretched across the stream.

What Is Man, That Thou Art Mindful Of Him?

In outer space the awestruck mind beholds
Vast galaxies in ranks beyond surmise;
Each spiral scarf of clustered light unfolds
More stars, ablaze and myriad in the skies.

Of all this host, some fate elected one
To be the source of life and light for man;
And of the spheres that wheel around the sun
God chose our humble planet for His plan.

And here, upon the cooling crust of earth,
Life, the miracle, began its climb
Until the human soul was given birth
Out of the nothingness of timeless time.

O what is man, in all this boundless space,
That Thou hast made his heart
Thy dwelling place?

My Son

His cry of anguish stabbed me like a knife;
  My son, my infant son, with gasping breath,
Lay clinging to the dying spark of life.
  A child-heart faltering at the gate of death.

We watched the candle flicker through the night;
  And when the doctor rose and shook his head,
I fought the tears of grief with lips pressed tight;
  The world turned black and all my hopes
    were dead.

And then I prayed, pinning my faith on One
  Who bears the sorrows of humanity.
I prayed to Him — Who also loved His Son
  And knew the heartbreak of Gethsemane.

And as I prayed, the breath of life returned;
  The son I loved came back from death's
    dark door.
And then I wept, with pent-up tears that burned,
  And gave myself to Him forevermore.

Upsala College
Library
East Orange, N. J.

Christmas Symphony

On Christmas eve I crossed a bridge
   That links two lands in amity.
No barrier stands across the span;
   Instead, my heart rejoiced to see
A portal arch of balsam boughs
   To spell once more, in tender light,
The starry words of peace and hope
   That shepherds heard one ageless night.

Afar I heard the church bells ring
   And saw the twinkling lights aglow;
A warming gladness filled the air
   As on that night of long ago;
And now, to join the symphony,
   The span and towers, climbing high,
Are like a lute-strung frame of song,
   A gleaming harp against the sky.

Both dreams of man invoke the stars:
   The bridge of faith, the prayerful spire;
Both give their anthems to the world
   To ring out with the heavenly choir;
And as their music soars aloft
   I hear the angel-song again,
The blessèd tidings of great joy:
   Peace on earth, good will to men.

A Bridge Of Peace

In human heart was born the plan:
A bridge of peace, uniting man.
Our sons will have the span we wrought;
The world the dream for which we fought.

Our Song Lives On

The torch we kindle burns throughout the night
  And in its flame we dare to dream again.
With dartling rays of kindness, love and light,
  We build a heaven in the hearts of men.

We hear the call of music and aspire
  To dwell in beauty where no beauty is.
Our voices join the paradisal choir
  Whose anthem wakes immortal harmonies.

We breach the walls of this too transient hour
  And voyage still, beyond the bourn of space.
Our song, undying, mounts the topmost tower
  And makes enduring music for the race.

Out Of The Fog

The foghorn blasts the night in mournful tone
And passing ships sound horns in hoarse reply,
Each veiled in swirling mist, afar, alone.

Impenetrable fog blots out the sky
And cloaks the sea with chilling clouds of doom,
A world in shrouds as though about to die.

Beyond the rocks the ghost-ships dimly loom,
Each blinded bark in moaning call, forlorn,
With black-veiled waters waiting to entomb.

    Across the dark the wailing sounds are borne;
    The stars are dead, the earth remains
        to mourn.

Into the rolling fog the seamen stare
At lights that blur and quickly fade away,
Leaving the ships to grope against despair.

The brave of heart can only hope and pray
For end of night and perils that surround.
At last a rose-hued dawn unveils the day.

And then the sun breaks through. In glad rebound
Beneath blue skies, all hearts rejoice to see
God's world so beautiful, with sunlight crowned.

Out of the fog of night, from darkness free,
With hope reborn, all men give thanks to Thee.

So Little Dost Thou Ask Of Me

How beautiful my garden grows,
　So grateful for a little care;
I thrill to see each budding rose
　With fragrance like a thankful prayer.

The meager breadcrumbs I supply,
　How joyously the birds repay:
On topmost boughs against the sky
　They sing for me the livelong day.

And when I try to do my part
　To spread some kindliness and cheer,
A flood of sunlight fills my heart;
　I hear a whisper, God is near!

O Lord, for all Thy boundless grace,
　So little dost Thou ask of me:
To make a simple dwelling place,
　A corner in my heart for Thee.

Journey's End

With life's full meed of dreams fulfilled,
   of love and laughter,
I have known Heaven here. If there is
   more hereafter,
I do not fret impatiently to know; nor weep
If journey's end is but a long surcease in sleep.

The road was long and steep before I reached
   the crest
With risen evening star to bid me pause and rest;
So weary children, after playing in the sun,
Are softly called to home and sleep, when day
   is done.

I linger on a grassy knoll; a woodbird sings
And twilight brings the hushed caress of
   mystic wings.
I am content to sleep. I do not ask to see
Beyond the canopy of stars spread over me.

Flight

With thunder of ten thousand fiery steeds
Our gleaming chariot leaps to skyward flight.
Through blue-domed space our wingèd
    transport speeds
Above the cumulus of drifting white.
We leave behind the tumult of the crowds;
The muffled engine-throb is all we hear.
In sunlit peace we fly above the clouds
And find release from earthbound storm and fear.

With trust in pilot and his star-mapped plan
We wing our way to gain our sunset goal.
This magic power of flight achieved by man
Fulfills an age-long dream within his soul,
Setting his vexed but eager spirit on
To seek a brighter day, a rosier dawn.

The Dreamer

His dream ship floats on seas of amethyst
And leaves a wake of star-flamed sapphire foam.
The Dreamer stands on deck in lonely tryst
Under the mantle of the purple dome.
As soft winds stir the sails to beckoning goals,
The ship sways gently toward one side and then,
To lullaby of cradling waves, it rolls
In even cadence slowly back again.

The Dreamer sees the gleaming stars appear
In downward swing, until they seem to be
Almost within his reach, they loom so near,
Only to draw away to apogee.
He may not grasp the stars as they pass by,
But sadder far would be a starless sky.

For Every Sorrow

(to Renée)

When I was vexed with care and strain,
  My solace was your tenderness.
For every sorrow, every pain,
  Your love was there, to heal and bless.

When years of thankless toil slipped past,
  I found my guerdon in your eyes;
And when life's laurels came at last,
  Your tears of gladness were my prize.

A Christmas Sleigh Ride

When love was young and hearts were gay,
  Who minded wintry weather?
All snugly bundled in the sleigh
  We sallied forth together.

When cheeks were flushed and lips were warm,
  Who minded snowflakes clinging?
Our joy rang out above the storm
  In tune with sleigh bells ringing.

Through sunset glow and first star-bright,
  What brought the tender yearning?
We glided home toward candlelight
  And warmth of Yule logs burning.

Compulsion

I cannot write a poem, dear,
    But since it is your sweet command
That I must rhyme to bring you cheer,
    I let my heartbeats guide my hand.

An earthborn clod, I often nod
    When I essay a verse or two.
The only perfect poet is God:
    He wrought his poetry in you.

This Gladness I Have Known

I have seen a bluebird on the wing
    Above a field in gold and scarlet hue;
A spray of apple blossoms in the spring
    In shimmering light against a sky of blue.

I have known the joy of perfect days,
    A grassy bank, a stream in jeweled glow;
Then oak and maple leaves in autumn blaze,
    And pines in winter, aureoled in snow.

Night-Blooming Water Lily

Lily, refulgent in petals of white,
Fair ballerina, enchanting the night,
Kissed by the moonlight, you slowly unfold
Beauty, in bodice of velvet and gold.

Motionless . . . quivering . . . held in a trance . . .
Dew-spangled, twinkling like stars in your dance,
Raptured, you sway to the nightingale's tune,
Turning your face to your lover, the moon.

Easter In My Garden

On Easter morn, with reverent hush,
   My garden greets the dawn's first ray;
Then, high aloft, a lilting thrush
   Acclaims with joy the newborn day.

The leaves and blossoms, dewy bright,
   Are framed against a dome of blue,
Like stained-glass windows, tinting light
   In slanting rays of jeweled hue.

The benediction streaming down
   Now gilds the trembling leaves with fire,
While birds in vestments red and brown
   Alight on boughs to form a choir.

They sing the joy of all the earth
   On spring's return to field and grove;
They sing the hymn of life's rebirth:
   God lives to fill the world with love.

Winter Sunset

I leap upon my horse and dash away
  Past farms and orchards blanketed with snow;
I race against the softly fading day
  To gain the heights suffused in afterglow.

Through fragrant forest aisles we slow our pace
  Where tall crowned pines and balsams
    make their stand;
The snow-heaped hemlock branches brush my face
  As I survey a winter wonderland.

Dismounting near the summit of my quest,
  I climb the ridge until my goal is won;
With pounding heart I pause upon the crest
  And view the glory of the dying sun.

Then homeward bound I give my horse the rein;
  He lopes along beneath the starry dome.
He sniffs familiar air and speeds once more
  In one last gallop toward the lights of home.

The Challenge

Nature said: "You cannot."
   Man replied: "I can."
From shore to shore, above the tides,
   He built a gleaming span.

Nature said: "You dare not."
   Man replied: "I dare."
He launched his wingèd ship aloft
   And boldly sailed the air.

Nature said: "You shall not."
   Man replied: "I will."
He caged the thunderbolts of Jove
   And made them serve his skill.

Nature said: "You must not."
   Man replied: "I must."
He split the atom. Now he holds
   A godlike power in trust.

Of this first printing of *I Built a Bridge & Other Poems*, fifteen hundred copies were printed on Rising Interlace by The Davidson Press of New York in the month of July 1955